Super Space Science

BEYOND THE SOLAR SYSTEM

David Hawksett

$$d = \sqrt{(x_2 - x_1) + (y_2 - y_1)^2}$$

Raintree is an imprint of Capstone Global Library Limited, a company incorporated in England and Wales having its registered office at 264 Banbury Road, Oxford, OX2 7DY - Registered company number: 6695582

www.raintree.co.uk
myorders@raintree.co.uk

Text © Capstone Global Library Limited 2019
The moral rights of the proprietor have been asserted.

Produced for Raintree by Calcium
Edited by Sarah Eason
Designed by Paul Myerscough
Picture research by Rachel Blount
Originated by Capstone Global Library Limited © 2018

ISBN 978 1 4747 6574 9 (hardback)
22 21 20 19 18
10 9 8 7 6 5 4 3 2 1

ISBN 978 1 4747 6589 3 (paperback)
23 22 21 20 19
10 9 8 7 6 5 4 3 2 1

British Library Cataloguing in Publication Data
A full catalogue record for this book is available from the British Library.

Acknowledgements
We would like to thank the following for permission to reproduce photographs: Cover: Shutterstock: Cigdem bg, Elenarts center; Inside: NASA: NASA/ESA/G. Bacon 36–37, NASA and the Night Sky Network 23b; Shutterstock: Cigdem 6–7, 44tl, Designua 31cr, Guzel Studio 27cr, Victor Habbick 42, Basti Hansen 32–33 bg, Tragoolchitr Jittasaiyapan 20–21, 44bl, Georgios Kollidas 32, 45cl, Lunatictm 27tr, Jurik Peter 35, Bruce Rolff 43, Vadim Sadovski 30–31, Tale 33; Wikimedia Commons: Rogelio Bernal Andreo 19, ESA/NASA/L. Calcada (ESO for STScI) 1, 34, ESO/L. Calcada 38–39, ESO/DSS 2 16–17, NASA 13, NASA/CXC/M. Weiss 17b, 25, NASA/ESA/G. Bacon (STScI) 18, NASA/ESA, A. Feild/STScI 15, NASA/ESA/J. Hester/A. Loll (Arizona State University) 24, NASA/ESA/M. Kornmesser (ESO) 10–11, NASA/ESA/M. Robberto (Space Telescope Science Institute/ESA)/Hubble Space Telescope Orion Treasury Project Team 22–23, NASA/ESA/The Hubble Heritage Team (STScI/AURA) 29b, NASA/Goddard Conceptual Image Lab 41, 45bl, NASA's Goddard Space Flight Center/NAOJ 37t, NASA/JHU APL/SWRI 4, NASA/JHU APL/SwRI/Steve Gribben 8, NASA/Jjron 9, NASA/JPL 4–5, 40, NASA/JPL-Caltech 12–13, Davide Papalini 10br, PlanetUser 39b, Emil Eugen Sachse 14, 44cl, NASA/CXC/MIT/L.Lopez et al. (x-ray)/NSF/NRAO/VLA (radio)/Palomar (infrared) 26, 45tl, Detlef Hartmann (optical)/NASA/CXC/SAO (x-ray)/NASA/JPL-Caltech (infrared) 28–29.

Every effort has been made to contact copyright holders of material reproduced in this book. Any omissions will be rectified in subsequent printings if notice is given to the publisher.

All the internet addresses (URLs) given in this book were valid at the time of going to press. However, due to the dynamic nature of the internet, some addresses may have changed, or sites may have changed or ceased to exist since publication. While the author and publisher regret any inconvenience this may cause readers, no responsibility for any such changes can be accepted by either the author or the publisher.

Printed in China.

CONTENTS

Chapter 1
INTERSTELLAR SPACE

Space is called "space" for a reason: Most of it is just space! The distances between objects in space can be mind-boggling. The distances between objects in our **solar system** alone are huge. For example, if you wanted to go from Earth to the Sun, you would need to travel 150 million kilometres. From the Sun to its nearest planet, Mercury, is 55 million kilometres. Mars is 228 million kilometres from the Sun. The area of space between the Sun and Mars is called the inner solar system.

The outer solar system

The space after Mars is the outer solar system. It includes a belt of millions of asteroids, each **orbiting** the Sun. Then, we come to Jupiter, the first of the **gas giants**. As we journey further beyond the edge of our solar system, we enter a huge, never-ending area of space. We call this interstellar space. "Interstellar" means "between the stars".

This is a photo of Pluto and its large moon, Charon, taken by the **New Horizons** spacecraft as it approached Pluto in July 2015.

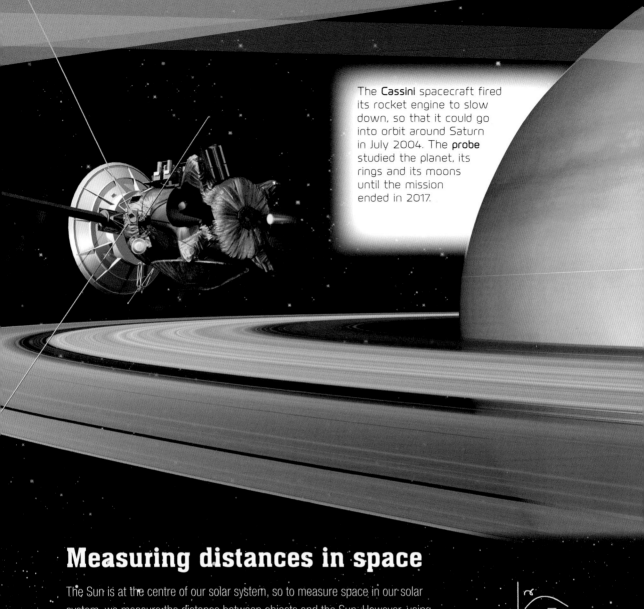

The **Cassini** spacecraft fired its rocket engine to slow down, so that it could go into orbit around Saturn in July 2004. The **probe** studied the planet, its rings and its moons until the mission ended in 2017.

Measuring distances in space

The Sun is at the centre of our solar system, so to measure space in our solar system, we measure the distance between objects and the Sun. However, using kilometres to measure these distances can be difficult because the numbers are much too large.

Instead, we use the speed of light to measure distance in space. The speed of light is how fast light travels from one place to another. At 299,792 kilometres per second, light travels from Earth to the Moon in about 1.5 seconds. So we can say the Moon is around 1.5 light-seconds away. Sometimes, scientists convert light-seconds into

$$\sqrt{(x_1 - x_2)^2 + (y_a - y_1)^2}$$

MEASURING OUR SOLAR SYSTEM

The distance between planets in our solar system and the Sun can also be measured in **light-years**. Take a look at these measurements in the table below.

If this illustration of the solar system was to the correct scale, the planets would just be tiny dots visible only through a microscope.

Distance between the Sun and the solar system planets using the speed of light:

Mercury	193 light-seconds or 3.2 light-minutes
Venus	360 light-seconds or 6 light-minutes
Earth	499 light-seconds or 8.3 light-minutes
Mars	759 light-seconds or 12.6 light-minutes
Jupiter	2,595 light-seconds or 43.2 light-minutes
Saturn	4,759 light-seconds or 79.3 light-minutes
Uranus	9,575 light-seconds or 159.6 light-minutes
Neptune	14,998 light-seconds or 4.1 light-hours

Now that we have seen the distances in light-seconds, it would be useful to see the measurements in a **scale model**.

Be a space scientist!

Create a scale model of the solar system.

You will need:

1 football pitch
9 small flags
1 x 5 pence piece
2 x 10 pence pieces
2 x 1 pence pieces

Instructions

1. Put your 5 pence on the goal line. This is the Sun. Mark it with a flag.
2. Each flag represents a planet. Write each planet's name on a flag. Place your planets as follows:
   - Mercury is 70 centimetres from the goal line. The inner planets at this scale are around the size of grains of sand, so we will place flags to represent their positions.
   - Place your flag for Venus at 1.3 metres from the Sun.
   - Earth is 1.8 metres from the Sun.
   - Mars is 2.7 metres from the Sun.
3. So far, we have not travelled far from the goal line. But now we are entering the outer solar system and can see the distances increase.
4. Place your Jupiter flag 9.6 metres from the Sun. Next to it, place one of your 10 pence pieces in the ground, so its edge points up. The coin's thickness is the size of Jupiter.
5. Saturn is 17.3 metres from the Sun. Use another vertical 10 pence piece to show its size.
6. Plant the Uranus flag 34.7 metres from the Sun, and put a 1 pence piece next to it. The planet is the same size as a letter on the coin!
7. Put a 1 pence piece down for Neptune 24.3 metres from the Sun. Again, one of the coin's letters shows its size.

$$x_1) + (y_2 - y_1)^2$$

TRAVELLING INTO SPACE

It takes a huge amount of **energy** to travel from Earth into space. Objects are held to Earth by its **gravity**. To escape gravity, a vehicle must travel forwards with huge **force** and speed. Rockets are powerful vehicles that can move with great force and speed. They are used to travel into space. The development of modern-day rockets began during World War II (1939–1945).

Rocket power

In 1944, towards the end of World War II, Germany developed the V-2 "Vengeance" rocket. It was launched from **mainland** Europe to bomb London. On 20 June 1944, a V-2 test flight reached 175 kilometres high. The distance from the surface of Earth to space is 100 kilometres, so the V-2 weapon became the first man-made object to enter space.

After the war ended, scientists began putting space probes on top of rockets. By 1957, the Union of Soviet Socialist Republics (USSR) had used a rocket to put *Sputnik 1* into orbit around Earth.

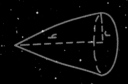

This artist's impression of **New Horizons** passing Pluto was made before astronomers knew what Pluto looked like.

Space Shuttle **Discovery** with a crew of seven astronauts blasts off to the International Space Station (ISS) on 23 October 2007.

To do this, they needed to get into space, but they also needed to reach a speed of more than 27,359 kilometres an hour. This meant that rockets had to become larger and more powerful. In the 1960s, the United States and the USSR began sending rockets carrying space probes to the planets.

Exploring planets

The first probes to the planets were simple **flybys**. They had only one chance to take as many pictures as possible, as they hurtled past Venus and Mars at thousands of kilometres an hour. The next probes could enter orbit around their targets. This meant that they could study them for months, rather than hours. In 2015, the New Horizons mission to Pluto showed us this icy part of the solar system in detail for the first time. To date, we have explored all the planets in our solar system, as well as its asteroids and comets. But what lies beyond this, in interstellar space?

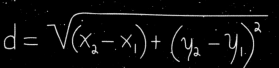

$$d = \sqrt{(x_2 - x_1) + (y_2 - y_1)^2}$$

Chapter 2
MEASURING THE UNIVERSE

Do you think the solar system is big? The distances between the planets may be vast, but the distances between the stars in interstellar space are even greater! It took astronomers more than 1,000 years to realize just how far apart the stars are.

Ancient astronomers

The first person to work out that the Sun and stars were the same type of object was the Greek **philosopher**, Anaxagoras. He lived from about 510 to 428 BC and was fascinated by the things he saw in nature. He tried to explain **shooting stars**, rainbows, **eclipses**, the Sun and other stars. The stars, he said, were fiery stones like the Sun. He noted that we do not feel their heat because they are so much further away than our star, the Sun. As for the Sun itself, he described it as a fiery mass bigger than the Peloponnese. This is a region of Greece that is 21,549 square kilometres in area.

Italian astronomer Giordano Bruno (1548-1600) believed there was no centre to the universe.

$$d = \sqrt{(x_2 - x_1) + (y_2 - y_1)^2}$$

This artist's impression shows Bruno's universe. Planets are common instead of rare, and different solar systems have different sizes and numbers of planets. Once again, the planet sizes are not to scale.

In the 16th century, Giordano Bruno announced that he believed the stars were like the Sun but further away. He said he thought they even had their own planets, on which other forms of life might be found. At the time, the Catholic Church forbade such thoughts, and Bruno was burned to death for his beliefs.

The nearest stars

In 1838, German astronomer Friedrich Bessel (1784–1846) became the first person to measure accurately the distance from Earth to another star. He calculated the exact positions of the more than 50,000 stars in the sky using a device called a **meridian circle**. With this information, he used a method known as **parallax** to measure the distance to one of the nearest stars, 61 Cygni. His result was 10.3 light-years, which is not bad, considering that today, we know this distance is 11.4 light-years. This is more than 700,000 times further than the Sun is from Earth! Do you still think the solar system is big?

BEYOND OUR GALAXY

Stars in the universe clump together in huge groups called **galaxies**. The word "galaxy" comes from the Greek word **galaxias**, which means "milky". The stars in the night sky are not evenly spaced. On a clear night, away from street lights, a faint band of milky light can be seen crossing the whole sky. Italian astronomer Galileo Galilei (1564–1642) was the first to realize that this band of light was made up of countless stars. We call this band the Milky Way.

Our nearest big galaxy, the Andromeda galaxy, is 2.2 million light-years away. This image was taken in ultraviolet (UV) light, which highlights the hottest stars in this spiral galaxy.

$$d = \sqrt{(x_2 - x_1) + (y_2 - y_1)^2}$$

A universe of galaxies

Until the 1920s, people believed that all the stars in the universe were within our galaxy. But astronomers had observed strange clouds in space, known as nebulae, which seemed to be outside our galaxy. In 1919, US astronomer Edwin Hubble (1889–1953) began working with the giant 254-centimetre wide Hooker Telescope. He studied some of these nebulae and was able to see that some, if **magnified** enough, seemed to be made of stars. Hubble had discovered the rest of the universe beyond our galaxy!

Beyond the Milky Way

The Milky Way contains as many as 400 billion stars. The nearest star to the Sun, Proxima Centauri, is only 4.25 light-years from Earth. It would take a journey of at least 100,000 light-years to cross from one side of our galaxy to the other. Since Hubble's discovery, we now know the nearest big galaxy to our own, the Andromeda Galaxy, is about 2.2 million light-years away. More powerful telescopes, including the Hubble Space Telescope (named after Edwin Hubble), have discovered that the universe contains at least 2 trillion galaxies!

This picture of the Hubble Space Telescope was taken by astronauts on the space shuttle **Discovery** in February 1997.

THE STARS

When Friedrich Bessel measured the distance to a nearby star in 1838, he used the parallax method. It is a good method but works only when measuring distances to the nearest stars in the Milky Way because the movements of distant stars cannot be easily seen. To experiment with the parallax method, all you need are two eyes and one finger.

$$d = \sqrt{(x_2 - x_1) + (y_2 - y_1)^2}$$

Astronomy with your finger

If you hold up one finger at arm's length and then close one eye, you can see your finger in the foreground and everything else in the background. If you then close that eye and open the other, your finger appears to have moved against the background. It has not really moved; you are just viewing it from a slightly different angle. Try this again, but put your finger much closer to your face. You should be able to see that your finger seems to have moved more against the background than before.

Bessel worked for a shipping company at the age of 14. He learned maths and navigation to help with the ships' journeys. This led him to a lifelong passion for astronomy.

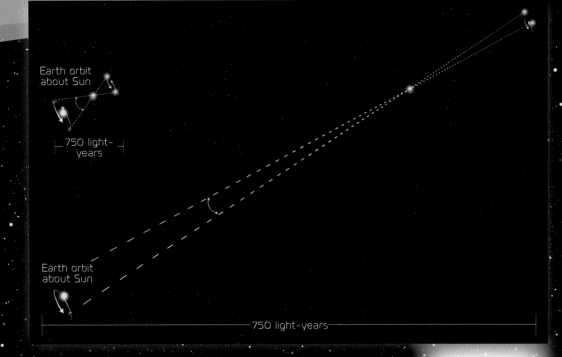

Earth orbit
about Sun

750 light-
years

Earth orbit
about Sun

750 light-years

Parallax

Using the method explained on page 14, imagine that your finger is a nearby star and the background is made up of more distant stars. Then imagine that your nose is the Sun and your eyes are different positions of Earth in its orbit. Instead of closing one eye and then the other, measure the position of the star (your finger) against the background, and then do exactly the same six months later. Earth will then be on the opposite side of the Sun to where it was before. Nearby stars will seem to have moved during that time. We know the size of Earth's orbit, so we can calculate the distance to the star by how much it moved.

The Hubble Space Telescope uses a technique called spatial scanning, which makes using parallax even more precise. Astronomers can now measure distances to the stars ten times further away.

Be a space scientist!

From what you have learned, can you remember why parallax works only for stars that are nearby?

Chapter 3
LOOKING AT THE STARS

Stars can be many different sizes and colours. They can have different temperatures and **life spans**. The colours of the stars depend on how hot they are. The reddest stars are the coolest. The bluest stars are the hottest. The table below shows how we classify, or organize, stars.

One of our nearest stars is Alpha Centauri.

Star colours and their temperatures

Star colour	Temperature in degrees C	Temperature in degrees F
Class O blue	Hotter than 30,000	54,032
Class B blue-white	10,000–30,000	18,032–54,032
Class A white	7,500–10,000	13,532–18,032
Class F yellow-white	6,000–7,500	10,832–13,532
Class G yellow	5,200–6000	9,392–10,832
Class K orange	3,700–5,200	6,692–9,392
Class M red	2,400–3,700	4,352–6,692

To remember this information, some people use a mnemonic device that makes a sentence out of initials from the star colour initials. A favorite mnemonic is "Oh Be A Fine Girl/Guy, Kiss Me".

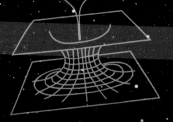

Our star

Our Sun is a yellow star with a classification of G. That makes it a fairly common star, but it is unusual in other ways. One of the nearest stars to the Sun, Alpha Centauri, is made up of two stars that orbit each other. A star made up of two stars is called a binary star, and a star made up of three stars is called a triple star. Proxima Centauri, the nearest star to the Sun, may be orbiting Alpha Centauri. That would make it a triple star system. In fact, about 85 per cent of all stars in our galaxy are binary stars, triple or even quadruple (four) star systems. Astronomers have even discovered a handful of systems that contain six or seven stars orbiting each other, but these are very rare.

Changing stars

Some stars change over short periods of time in a predictable way. Cepheid variable stars can be 20 times heavier than the Sun and 100,000 times brighter. Over just a few days, some of these stars grow and shrink by up to one-quarter of their width.

This artist's impression shows a planet orbiting so closely to a massive red giant star that its atmosphere is slowly being stripped away.

$$d = \sqrt{(x_2 - x_1) + (y_2 - y_1)^2}$$

MONSTER STARS

As well as colour and temperature, the size of the stars also varies greatly. Our Sun is roughly in the middle of the star colour ranges. It measures 1,391,399 kilometres across. This is about 109 times the width of Earth. The Sun could hold about 1,300,000 Earths inside its volume, or total space.

Giant stars

The brightest star in the night sky, Sirius, is a white class A star. It is bright because it is close to Earth, at just 8.6 light-years away. It is about twice as heavy as the Sun and nearly twice the width. If you look at the bright star, Betelgeuse, in the **constellation** of Orion, you will see a star very different from our Sun. It is a **red supergiant**. Betelgeuse is 643 light-years away and is bright because it is so large. Betelgeuse's width is estimated to be about 766,700,000 kilometres: That is about 890 times wider than the Sun.

This is what the binary system, Sirius, would look like to visiting humans. The bright white A-class main star outshines its companion, Sirius B, which became a white dwarf star about 120 million years ago.

A galactic monster

One of the largest stars that we know of is called VY Canis Majoris. It is found in the constellation Canis Major. This is a monster star known as a red **hypergiant**. Its width is about 1,227,400,000 kilometres, which means you could fit 1,420 Suns across its **diameter**. It is also about 17 times heavier than the Sun and gives out 270,000 times more light. This star is so large that if you removed the Sun and swapped it for VY Canis Majoris, it would swallow all the inner solar system planets, the asteroid belt and Jupiter. To try to grasp its size, imagine flying over the surface of the star in an aeroplane. Flying around Earth would take about 40 to 50 hours. Flying around VY Canis Majoris would take an incredible 1,100 years!

The three stars that make up Orion's belt are in the centre. At the upper left and bottom right are the supergiant stars, Betelgeuse and Rigel. The orange colour of Betelgeuse is obvious even with the naked eye.

$$d = \sqrt{(x_2 - x_1) + (y_2 - y_1)^2}$$

COMPARING STARS

The model of the solar system on page 7 showed us the scale of the planets compared to the Sun. Now, we will make a scale model to show the size of our solar system compared to the nearest stars. These include Proxima Centauri, which is just 4.25 light-years away and is nearest to the Sun. However, it is a **red dwarf** and cannot be seen without a telescope. Alpha Centauri is also near Earth. This triple star system is 4.37 light-years away, which is further away than Proxima Centauri. However, because it is much larger than our Sun, it can be seen shining brightly with the help of a telescope.

Alpha Centauri can only ever be seen from Earth's southern hemisphere. It never rises above the horizon in the north. Alpha Centauri A and B are slightly bigger and slightly smaller than the Sun respectively. Proxima Centauri is too faint to be seen with the naked eye.

$$d = \sqrt{(x_2 - x_1)} + (y_2 - y_1)^2$$

Be a space scientist!

In the scale model of the solar system on page 7, we shrank the Sun and the eight planets to fit into a football pitch. Now, imagine shrinking the solar system so that we can fit in Alpha Centauri, too.

You will need:

Ruler
Sheet of paper
1 football pitch
2 marker flags

Scissors
Binoculars
Glue or tape

Instructions

1. Using the ruler, measure 1.1 cm from a corner of the sheet of paper. Cut out a square this size, 1.1 cm along each side. Trim it to make it roughly circular, and do the same again using another corner of the sheet of paper.

2. Use the glue or tape to stick one of your tiny paper circles to a flag. This circle is the whole solar system. You would need a microscope to see the Sun or any of the planets in it! Put your solar system on the goal line.

3. Now walk to the other goal line, and stick the other paper circle to the other flag. Place it on the ground. This is the Alpha Centauri system.

4. Now try to find your flag with the binoculars. Can you see it? You are an imaginary astronomer on a planet orbiting Alpha Centauri. How much could you learn about our solar system using your binoculars (telescope) from Alpha Centauri?

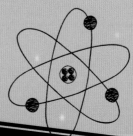

Chapter 4
THE LIFE OF A STAR

Nothing lasts forever, not even the Sun and the other stars. The Sun is about 4.6 billion years old, but the universe is roughly 13.8 billion years old. So how did the Sun and the stars come to exist? Dotted throughout our Milky Way galaxy are nebulae. These are the places where stars are born. If you look in the constellation of Orion, you can see one of the most famous nebulae. Below the three bright stars that make up Orion's Belt, there are three much fainter stars. They make up Orion's sword, which hangs from the belt. The middle of the three sword stars appears slightly fuzzy to the naked eye. This is not a star: It is the Orion Nebula.

A starry nursery

The Orion Nebula is a huge cloud of gas and dust that measures 24 light-years across. It is about 1,344 light-years from Earth. Inside the nebula is a cluster of about 1,000 stars. These are only one million years old. We now know that these stars formed inside the nebula from the gas and dust there. Nebulae are sometimes called "star nurseries" because lots of baby stars form there.

Below Orion's belt is the Great Nebula of Orion. This close-up view shows the patterns of gas and dust in this region of space where stars are forming. Some of the brightest stars in the middle are about 300,000 years old, and some could be much younger.

Making stars

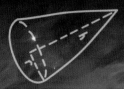

Stars are created from enormous explosions of energy. When a giant star explodes, it sends a **shock wave** through space. The huge explosion is called a **supernova**. The **shock wave** can cause the gas and dust in a nebula to be squeezed so forcefully and with such **pressure** that the nebula starts to collapse. As it shrinks, it becomes hotter and hotter. Its gas and dust start to spin around. Eventually, it becomes so hot at the centre of the nebula that the gas ignites, or catches fire, in a **nuclear reaction**. It becomes a shining star. The rest of the gas and dust in the nebula flattens out into a spinning disc. Planets then form from this disc. The process can take millions of years. This is exactly what is happening in the Orion Nebula now.

This diagram shows the stages stars go through during their lifetime. A huge star dies in a supernova explosion. Normal-size stars die more slowly. They swell into a giant red star, then turn into a planetary nebula with a white dwarf star in the centre.

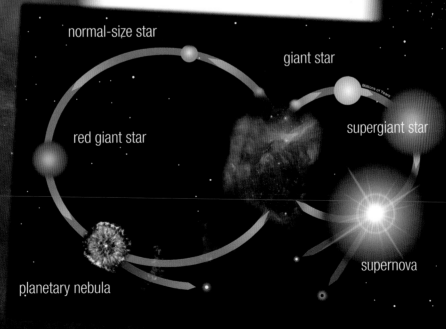

normal-size star

giant star

red giant star

supergiant star

Millions of Years

planetary nebula

supernova

$$d = \sqrt{(x_2 - x_1) + (y_2 - y_1)^2}$$

DEATH OF A STAR

Stars work by burning **hydrogen** in their cores. As it burns, the hydrogen changes into a gas called **helium**. It is helium that gives out the energy that makes a star shine. Hydrogen is a **fuel**, so what happens to a star when this fuel runs out?

Ordinary stars

In a common star like the Sun, when its hydrogen starts to run out, the star begins to shrink. This makes the core of the star hotter. This then heats up the upper layers of the star. They then begin to expand, or grow bigger. The star has become a red giant. Next, the helium begins to change into **carbon**. Once all the helium has changed into carbon, the star begins to cool into a white dwarf. The outer layers of the star drift off into space and form a planetary nebula. The white dwarf star that remains is about the same size as Earth. It will take billions of years to cool down enough to stop shining. One day, billions of years from now, this will happen to our Sun.

The Crab Nebula, in the constellation of Taurus, is the remains of a supernova. This cloud of gas is still growing as a result of the explosion that was seen in the sky in AD 1054.

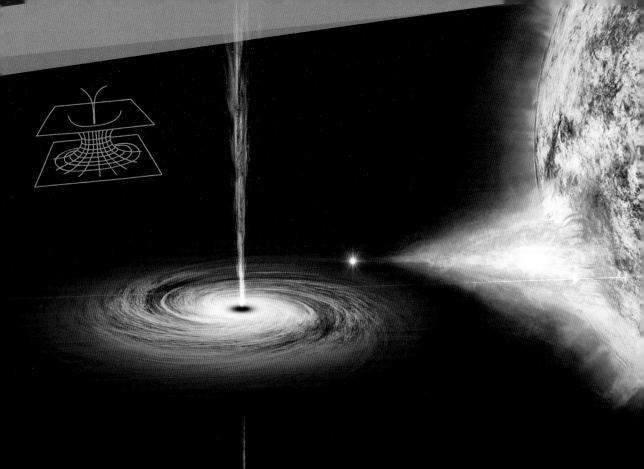

A black hole, Cygnus X1, is sucking gas from its companion, which forms a spinning disc around the black hole before being sucked into oblivion.

Monster stars

In much bigger stars, something more dramatic happens. After the helium changes into carbon, it becomes hot enough to change into many more **elements**. Eventually, the core runs out of elements that can make energy. Then, the star shuts down. All of a sudden, the star collapses under its own weight. This releases a shock wave that blows the entire star to pieces. It becomes a supernova, which can be as bright as an entire galaxy.

The remains of the star's core then become a **neutron star**. Neutron stars weigh about the same as the Sun, but they are only the size of a city. Some neutron stars spin thousands of times per second and give out natural flashes of **radiation**. These are known as pulsars. The biggest supernovae can leave behind a black hole. The gravity of a black hole is so great that not even light can escape from it.

SUPERNOVAE

Supernovae are the most spectacular events in the universe. These explosions have made many chemical elements, such as silver and gold. You can find out what happens in a supernova by completing the "Be a space scientist!" activity on the page opposite.

W49B is the remains of a supernova that is 26,000 light-years away. The supernova only occurred 1,000 years ago and may contain our galaxy's youngest black hole.

$$d = \sqrt{(x_2 - x_1) + (y_2 - y_1)^2}$$

Be a space scientist!

This demonstration will show you how the effects of the shock wave inside a star cause a supernova. Let's imagine the balls are the inside of a massive star. The tennis balls are the heavier stuff in the core, and the ping-pong balls are the lighter, outer layers of the star.

You will need:

10 people
10 tennis balls
10 ping-pong balls
A hard surface, such as a concrete or tile floor

Instructions

1. Ask each person to hold a tennis ball in one hand and a ping-pong ball in the other. Now start throwing the tennis balls up in the air and catching them. Gravity makes the balls come back down, and the energy you gave them by throwing them up fights against it. Throwing balls in the air represents the energy from **nuclear fusion** in the core pushing outwards.

2. Imagine that your star's core has just run out of elements that can make energy with nuclear fusion. This happens when the star starts to make iron in its core. All of a sudden, the core stops making heat, and the star's gravity makes it collapse.

3. Ask each person to hold both balls in the same hand, with the tennis ball at the bottom. Stand in a circle, with your friends holding out a hand in the middle, a metre above the ground. After a countdown, ask everyone to let go of both balls and allow gravity to take over. Now that the core has stopped making energy, what happens when the balls hit the ground? Using the information you have learned in this book, how do you think this is like a supernova?

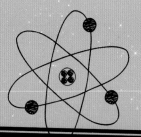

Chapter 5

A UNIVERSE OF GALAXIES

Galaxies are huge clusters of stars. They are clustered together because each star's gravity pulls it towards the stars nearest to it. Our galaxy, the Milky Way, is shaped like a spiral. It has a lot of arms and a **dense** core of old stars. Each of the 400,000,000,000 stars in our galaxy is orbiting the core. This type of galaxy makes up more than half of all galaxies.

Types of galaxy

Elliptical galaxies range from spherical to oval shaped. They make up about 1 in 10 of all galaxies in the universe. In spiral galaxies, all the stars orbit the centre in the same direction. In elliptical galaxies, they all follow their own random orbit. Elliptical galaxies can be much bigger than spiral galaxies. For example, IC 1101 could be about 5 million light-years across. That is about 50 times wider than the Milky Way. Roughly one-quarter of galaxies have no clear shape at all. The Small Magellanic Cloud is one of these galaxies. Some irregular galaxies have their shapes changed by the gravity of other nearby galaxies.

The beautiful spiral galaxy, M101, is 21 million light-years from our galaxy. M101 is 70 per cent bigger than our Milky Way.

Colliding galaxies

Some galaxies are large because they have "swallowed" other smaller galaxies. Andromeda, which is 2.2 million light-years away, is heading towards the Milky Way at 109 kilometres a second. In about four billion years, it will collide and merge with our galaxy. The collision will take millions of years, but the space between the stars is so great that no stars are expected to hit each other directly.

M82 is a starburst galaxy, which means it is undergoing an unusually high amount of star formation.

$$d = \sqrt{(x_2 - x_1) + (y_2 - y_1)^2}$$

THE EXPANDING UNIVERSE

In 1922–1923, Edwin Hubble discovered that "spiral nebulae" were actually other galaxies beyond the Milky Way. He discovered this by using a special method called "**standard candles**". In astronomy, a standard candle is any astronomical object that has a predictable brightness and size. On Earth, a standard candle could be something like a cow. We know all cows are about the same size, so you can tell how far away a cow is by how small it looks in a distant field. Hubble used the same idea to measure how far away stars are by studying their brightness. Hubble's discovery of very faint stars in the Andromeda spiral meant that they were far too distant to be in our own galaxy.

Getting bigger and bigger

Edwin Hubble is also famous for his work on the expansion of the universe. The idea of expansion can be seen in the **Doppler effect**, which is something we experience often. For example, sound waves coming from an approaching vehicle have a higher note than when the vehicle goes past you. This is because the sound waves are squeezed together while coming towards you and stretched out when moving away from you. The same thing happens with light. A star moving away will appear slightly redder, and it appears slightly bluer if approaching us. This is called "redshift". Hubble used redshift to measure the movement of other galaxies and found that they were all moving away from each other. The further the galaxy, the faster it was moving away. The only explanation for this was that the entire universe is expanding.

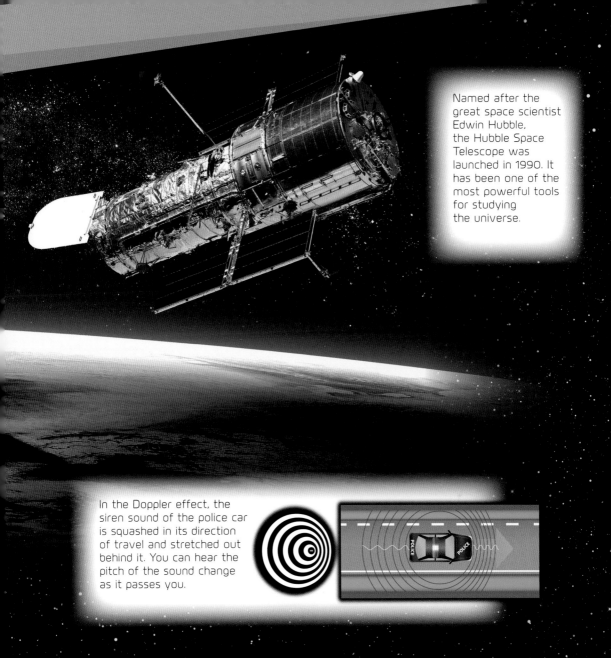

Named after the great space scientist Edwin Hubble, the Hubble Space Telescope was launched in 1990. It has been one of the most powerful tools for studying the universe.

In the Doppler effect, the siren sound of the police car is squashed in its direction of travel and stretched out behind it. You can hear the pitch of the sound change as it passes you.

The Big Bang

If the universe is growing in size, then you can imagine what it was like long ago. Galaxies must have been closer together than they are today. In fact, if you wind back time far enough, you can imagine all the galaxies being in the exact same place. That is what we now call the Big Bang, which is a point in time when all the **matter** in the universe came into being in one gigantic explosion.

$$d = \sqrt{(x_2 - x_1) + (y_2 - y_1)^2}$$

HUMANS AND THE UNIVERSE

$$d = \sqrt{(x_2 - x_1) + (y_2 - \ldots}$$

Our understanding of space has changed almost completely over the last 400 years. Up until then, most people believed that the Sun and everything else orbited the Earth. In 1610, Galileo Galilei looked at Jupiter and found four moons orbiting it. This was proof that not everything orbited Earth. In Italy at the time, it was against the law to question the Catholic Church's view that Earth was at the centre of the solar system and the universe. Galileo was put on trial by the Church in 1633. Despite being an old man, Galileo was sentenced to **house arrest** until his death in 1642.

Not at the centre?

We no longer think Earth is the center of the solar system. However, this can seem confusing if we consider that all the galaxies are moving away from ours. Is this not proof that we are at the centre of the universe? Find the answer to this question with the "Be a space scientist!" activity opposite.

Galileo looked at space through his early telescope. His many discoveries included mountains on the surface of the Moon.

The Milky Way contains as many as 400 billion stars. Our own Sun and planets are about halfway out from the centre, in what is known as the Orion Arm.

Be a space scientist!

You will need:

1 plain balloon with no air in it
1 black or blue pen
1 green pen

Instructions

Before you blow up the balloon, use the blue or black pen to cover it in dots; these represent galaxies. Make the dots the same size and roughly the same distance from each other. Use the green pen to mark one of the dots as our galaxy. Blow up the balloon in stages, with a break in between puffs. If you look at our galaxy (the green dot), you can see that all the dots closest to us have moved away. The ones furthest have moved even more. Now look at a dot (galaxy) other than ours. What has happened to it compared with what happened to our galaxy? Based on what you have seen, do you think there is a "centre" to the universe?

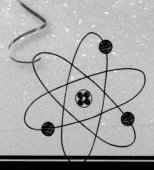

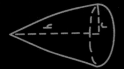

Chapter 6
LIFE IN THE UNIVERSE

The idea that other stars could have their own planets has been around for hundreds of years. Giordano Bruno suggested it in the 16th century. It is possible that our solar system was a blip, a malfunction in star formation, and something unique. This would make the universe a lonely place because life can take place only on a planet. In their search for other life in the universe, astronomers have been anxious to find other planets around other stars. We call these extrasolar planets, or "**exoplanets**" for short, so that we can tell them apart from our own planets.

The candle and the searchlight

Remember how far you had to walk from the solar system to reach Alpha Centauri in the activity on page 20? Now, imagine trying to spot our own planets from there. They are tiny compared to the Sun, which makes them very hard to see. Trying to see a tiny, dim planet when it is close to a dazzling shining star is like trying to spot a candle next to a powerful searchlight from far away. That is why astronomers use other methods to find exoplanets.

The planet Dagon is only 200 million years old. It orbits its star in a region filled with dust.

Finding exoplanets

$$d = \sqrt{(x_2 - x_1) + \left(y_2 - y_1\right)^2}$$

Seen from Earth, if a planet orbiting a star passes in front of it, the planet will block some of that star's light. That is one way that astronomers find other planets. Another way is through the "wobble method". Everything in space has gravity. The gravity of a planet orbiting a star pulls on the star, which makes it wobble very slightly. This wobble can be seen with powerful telescopes. In 1992, the very first exoplanet was found using the wobble method.

Planets everywhere

Since 1992, new methods for finding planets have been invented, and space telescopes have been launched just to look for exoplanets. Today, more than 3,500 exoplanets have been discovered in more than 2,500 star systems. It now seems that the universe is full of planets; our own galaxy probably has at least 100 billion of them. Thanks to these discoveries, the universe does not seem so lonely after all!

Gas giants are so much bigger than rocky planets that they make up most of the first exoplanets to be discovered. Like our own gas giants, these exoplanets are likely to have their own moons.

THE STRANGEST WORLDS

Now that we know planets are common, we know that we can find somewhere to land if we ever sent people out into the stars. What are these exoplanets like? Are there any like Earth that we could live on? Our planet orbits the Sun in what we call a "Goldilocks zone", after the fairy tale. A Goldilocks zone is an area in space in which a planet's distance from its Sun makes the planet neither too hot nor too cold, but just right.

Hot Jupiters

When looking for faint planets close to dazzling stars, you are most likely to discover the largest ones first. Gas giants, such as Jupiter and Saturn, are the easiest to find. However, many of these were not what astronomers expected to find. The gas giants orbit far from the Sun, with Jupiter taking 12 years to complete one orbit. Some exoplanets are called "hot Jupiters" because they are much closer to their stars than Jupiter. One planet, WASP 12-b, orbits its star 44 times closer than Earth orbits the Sun. It takes just over one Earth day (24 hours) to complete an orbit. Due to its closeness to the planet, the star's gravity pulls WASP 12-b into an egg shape. It even sucks gas from its **atmosphere**. This is an incredibly hot planet, where the temperature reaches 2, 200° C. It will probably be completely eaten by its star within 10 million years.

This image shows a "hot Jupiter" orbiting close to its parent star. The heat from the star can raise the temperature of these planets to thousands of degrees Celsius. The star's gravity can strip gas from the planet's atmosphere as it slowly eats it up!

$$d = \sqrt{(x_2 - x_1) + (y_2 - y_1)^2}$$

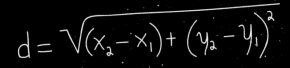

A study in 2013 showed that the gas methane is in Gliese 504 b's atmosphere. Enough is known about this planet to assume that it is magenta in colour.

Luke Skywalker's home?

Some exoplanets are unusual because of the stars they orbit. The very first one discovered actually orbits a pulsar, which is a city-size core formed in a supernova. The radiation from this pulsar would make this planet a dangerous place to visit. In 2011, the first planet was found orbiting a binary star. Like Tatooine, the planet in Star Wars, this world would have dramatic twin sunsets. However, what we really want to find is an Earth-like world – not too big or too small, not too hot or too cold, but just right.

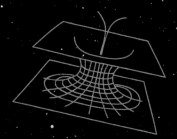

OUR NEIGHBOURS

Alpha Centauri and Proxima Centauri are the stars nearest to the Sun. Proxima is probably orbiting the binary stars of Alpha Centauri A and Alpha Centauri B. In 2015, astronomers revealed they had discovered a planet orbiting Alpha Centauri B. They found it using the Hubble Space Telescope. Named Alpha Centauri Bc, this planet is slightly smaller than Earth. Like Earth, it is rocky. It is too close to its star to support life, and its surface is probably made of **molten lava**. In 2016, it was discovered that Proxima Centauri, which is a red dwarf, also has a planet orbiting very close to it. However, radiation from the star means that humans could never live there.

Goldilocks zone

Just 23.6 light-years away is Gliese 667 C, a red dwarf star. Two planets have been found circling it. One is probably a small gas giant, like Neptune. However, this planet orbits too closely to its star to be **habitable**. The other is a rocky world that is bigger than Earth. This planet orbits right in the middle of the star's Goldilocks zone. It is probably locked in an orbit of its star, like the Moon is to Earth. That means that one half of the planet is always in sunlight, and the other half is in permanent darkness.

$$d = \sqrt{(x_2 - x_1) + (y_2 - y_1)^2}$$

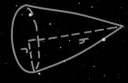

Earth-like worlds?

Gliese 665 Cb is a planet that is part of a triple star system. It is one of two planets discovered so far in this star system. Gliese 665 Cb is more than five times heavier than Earth.

Of all the exoplanets discovered so far, the one most like Earth is Kepler-438b, which is 470 light-years from Earth. Kepler-438b also orbits a star in the Goldilocks zone, and liquid water could exist on its surface. Its gravity and size are slightly greater than Earth's. The temperature at the surface is almost the same as on Earth. At first, Kepler-438b looked like the perfect planet for humans to visit. However, on further study, we now know that it has violent storms. It is also battered by flares from the star every 100 days or so. This alone would wipe out any life that tried to form on the planet.

Kepler 438b

Kepler 438b star

Kepler 438b is probably the most Earth-like exoplanet yet discovered, even though it could not support human life. It is slightly larger than Earth.

BUILDING A PROBE

Could you send a space **probe** to another star? Now that we know planets exist in our neighbouring star systems, we want to see them up close. How long would it take to reach another star?

Leaving the solar system

Voyager 2 is still working and sending back data to Earth about the conditions in deep space. Its battery is expected to keep it working until 2025.

The space probe *Voyager 2* was launched in 1977 and visited the four gas giants of the solar system. It took two years to reach Jupiter and did not fly by Neptune until 1989. *Voyager 2* and its twin, *Voyager 1,* are now far from the Sun. *Voyager 1* crossed the edge of the solar system in 2012 and became the first man-made object to enter interstellar space. In 300 years, it will reach the Oort cloud. This is a huge group of comets that orbit the Sun. *Voyager 1* will spend about 30,000 years passing through the cloud. In 40,000 years, it will pass the nearby star Gliese 445, which is 17.6 light-years away. *Voyager 2* will pass the bright star Sirius in 296,000 years.

Calling home

Both Voyager probes still have enough power to keep **transmitting** messages to Earth until the year 2025. The radio transmitter on the probes only has a power of 22.4 watts, which is about the same as the light bulb inside a refrigerator. By the time that radio signal has crossed the solar system to reach Earth, its power is 20 billion times less than a digital watch battery. NASA uses giant radio dishes on Earth to pick up this faint signal. Any probe that journeys to another star will need a much more powerful radio.

Be a space scientist!

In science fiction, people travel to other stars in just hours or minutes. In real life, however, we are limited to rockets, which push out hot fuel from one end to push a spacecraft in the other direction. It takes a lot of rocket fuel to get into space. When you see a rocket launch, only the tiny part at the top is the spacecraft. Most of the rocket is actually a fuel tank for the engines. Rockets are too inefficient to use on an interstellar mission. What kind of space-travel solutions can you think of that science fiction writers use? Do you think any of these fictional technologies might become real one day?

NASA's IBEX satellite was launched in 2008 and has been using its sensitive instruments to map the edge of the solar system. It was only supposed to last for 2 years, but it may last as long as 40.

$$d = \sqrt{(x_2 - x_1) + (y_2 - y_1)^2}$$

$$= \sqrt{(x_2 - x_1) + (y_2 - y_1)^2}$$

HUMANS TO THE STARS!

Once an interstellar space probe has arrived at an exoplanet, the probe will study the planet's surface and the chemistry of its air to see if it is breathable. It will then send that information back to Earth. Even moving at the speed of light, it will take years for this information to travel through interstellar space. Only when it reaches Earth will we know for certain if the planet could support human life. And only then can an interstellar mission to take people to another planet be planned.

A one-way trip

The Apollo missions to the Moon each had a crew of just three astronauts. A manned mission to Mars could have just six or so. The Moon and Mars are close enough to Earth for people to get there in days or months. They are also close enough for the astronauts to come home. Supply ships from Earth could transport any equipment needed to astronauts on Mars. However, an interstellar mission is likely to be a one-way trip. The travellers would need to take everything they need to survive the rest of their lives on the new planet.

An interstellar ship could have many different designs. All need to have a lot of room, not only for human occupants, but for all the supplies they would need for the journey.

A generation ship

We have not yet invented **warp drives** or **hyperdrives**. Nor do we have the faster-than-light engines that exist in science-fiction films. That means the journey to a distant planet will take a long time. A generation ship would carry enough people to have children during the trip to another planet. The journey to a faraway planet could take centuries. The original astronauts would grow old and die. However, their **descendants** would survive and reach the new planet. There, they could start a **colony**.

This illustration of a possible generation ship shows a large city built on the inside surface of a spinning tube. The spinning recreates the effect of gravity to make it more comfortable for the people inside.

Superpower!

During the 100-year-long flight of the generation ship, new technologies on Earth would be invented. They could even allow faster ships to catch up and overtake the generation ship. To get a spaceship to just one-tenth of the speed of light would take a massive amount of energy. All the energy consumed by all the people on Earth in a single afternoon would be used up. To make long-distance space travel possible, we need new, superpowerful engine technology. Perhaps one day, the person who invents it might be you!

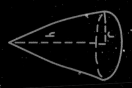

BE A SPACE SCIENTIST!
ANSWERS

Pages 6-7 Measuring our solar system

Congratulations! You have made a scale model of the solar system.

Pages 14-15 The stars

Parallax works only when measuring nearby stars because the movements of far more distant stars cannot be seen from Earth.

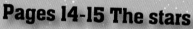

Pages 20-21 Comparing stars

Congratulations. You have made a scale model of the solar system and Alpha Centauri! Remember: the whole solar system is the size of the paper circle. Imagine shrinking your earlier solar system model down to that size. The planets and the Sun would need a microscope to be seen. From across the football pitch, you would be lucky if you even discovered that the Sun had planets orbiting it.

Pages 26-27 Supernovae

When you all let go of all the balls, gravity takes over, and they all fall towards the star's core (the ground). Try dropping the balls so that they all hit the ground next to each other and at the same time. The ping-pong balls (star's outer layers) go flying in all directions. This is like the shock wave that blows the star's outer layers into space.

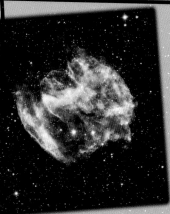

Pages 32-33 Humans and the universe

When you look at our galaxy on the balloon, it certainly seems that all the others are moving away from ours. But look at any other galaxy dot, and it seems that the others are moving away from that one! The only explanation is that there is no centre to the universe.

Pages 40-41 Building a probe

Science fiction and science fact share many ideas. Some sci-fi inspires scientific developments. Most stories set in space would be pretty dull if you set a course for a planet and then have to wait 10 years or more to get there! To get around this, science fiction writers use faster-than-light wormholes, warp drives and hyperdrives, which get you there much more quickly. Scientists today are even working on technologies that could do this in the future.

$$d = \sqrt{(x_2 - x_1)} + (y_2 - y_1)^2$$

GLOSSARY

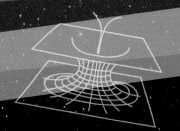

atmosphere blanket of gases that surrounds a planet

black hole region of space where the core of a massive star has collapsed to a size of zero with powerful gravity

carbon chemical element that diamonds and coal are made up of

colony place where a particular group of people lives

constellation shape in the night sky formed by a pattern of stars

dense closely packed

descendants people who come from the same family

diameter length of a straight line that can be drawn across a circular object, passing through the middle of it

Doppler effect squeezing and expanding of sound and light waves as a result of relative motion

eclipses when the Moon passes between Earth and the Sun, or Earth passes between the Moon and the Sun

elements basic materials from which everything is made

elliptical oval shaped

energy ability to do work

exoplanets planets in space that orbit a star other than the Sun

flybys close approach of a spacecraft to a planet or moon for observation

force push or pull that can change the way things move

fuel substance that reacts, usually by burning, to release a lot of heat, which can be used to power things

galaxies vast clusters of stars bound together by their own gravity

gas giants planets Jupiter, Saturn, Uranus and Neptune, which are made mainly of gas

gravity pull that any object has on any other. The bigger the object, or planet, the more gravity it has.

habitable describes a place where people and animals are able to live

helium gas that is lighter than air

house arrest when your house becomes your prison and you can never leave

hydrogen colourless, odourless, highly flammable gas

hyperdrives types of engine used in science fiction to allow people to travel faster than light

hypergiant biggest kind of star, which is even bigger than a supergiant

lava hot, molten rock that usually erupts from a volcano

life spans how long something is expected to live for

light-years unit of measurement for the distance light travels in one year

magnified made bigger

mainland biggest part of a country, rather than islands surrounding it

matter something that occupies space, has mass and can exist as a solid, liquid or gas

meridian circle special type of telescope for measuring star positions

molten melted or liquid

neutron star tiny, dead star core the size of a city, which is the remains of a supernova

nuclear fusion chemical reaction in which elements are turned into other elements

nuclear reaction process of changing elements, such as hydrogen, into heavier elements, such as helium

orbiting following a circular or oval path around an object in space as a result of the pull of the object's gravity

parallax method of measuring distances to things by looking at them from different angles

philosopher person who is a thinker and teacher

planetary nebula spherical cloud of gas and dust in space, formed by a dying star

pressure pushing force

probe unmanned spacecraft designed for exploration

$$d = \sqrt{(x_2 - x_1) + (y_2 - y_1)^2}$$

radiation energy that travels at the speed of light; includes visible light

red dwarf dim red star much smaller and fainter than the Sun

red supergiant massive red star hundreds of times bigger than the Sun

scale model imitation of an original object but smaller or bigger, using the same ratios

shock wave outside edge of an explosion

shooting stars dust particles from space burning up in Earth's atmosphere

solar system the Sun, its planets and moons, asteroids and comets

standard candles types of object in space that are always the same average brightness

supernova explosion at the end of a massive star's life

transmitting sending information back to a specific place

ultraviolet (UV) radiation with slightly shorter wavelengths than visible light. Naturally produced by the Sun.

warp drives type of engine that is used in science fiction, such as Star Trek, to travel in space faster than light

FIND OUT MORE

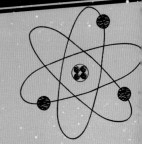

BOOKS

How to Be a Space Explorer: Your Out-Of-This-World Adventure, Mark Brake (Lonely Planet Kids, 2014)

How to Design the World's Best Space Station in 10 Simple Steps, Paul Mason (Wayland, 2016)

Jupiter and the Outer Planets (Astronaut Travel Guides), Andrew Solway (Raintree, 2014)

Spacecraft (Technology Timelines), Tom Jackson (Franklin Watts, 2016)

Space: The Whole Whizz-Bang Story (Science Sorted), Glenn Murphy (Macmillan Children's Books, 2014)

The Outer Planets (Space Travel), Giles Sparrow (Franklin Watts, 2014)

WEBSITES

DK Find Out More
www.dkfindout.com/uk/space/stars-and-galaxies/

Learn more facts and statistics about stars and galaxies, including how stars are born, what makes up a black hole and The Big Bang theory.

European Space Agency
www.esa.int/esaKIDSen/OurUniverse.html

Watch animations to learn more about the universe, discover how astronauts live in space and look at some of the technology that helps humans to explore space.

INDEX